PANDAS

by Michèle Dufresne

Pioneer Valley Educational Press, Inc.

The giant panda is a **mammal**. It is in the bear family.

The giant panda is an **endangered species**.

Once, there were many giant pandas living in the **wild**.

Today, scientists believe there are only a few thousand giant pandas living in the wild.

There are now places where pandas are protected from harm. Cutting down trees or bamboo in these special places is against the law. ▶

There are two kinds of pandas: giant pandas and red pandas.

Giant pandas are like bears. Red pandas are more like raccoons.

Giant pandas and red pandas like to eat **bamboo**.

Here is a red panda. It is slightly larger than a domestic cat.
Red pandas live in India and China. ▶

Giant pandas live in forests
in the mountains of China.

Their favorite food is bamboo.
There is a lot of bamboo
for the pandas to eat
in the mountains of China.

Pandas mostly eat bamboo. They also
will eat other plants and some meat. ▶

Giant pandas are
very large and strong.
They have black and white fur.
Their fur keeps them warm and dry.

Pandas grow to between
four and six feet in length.
They have long, sharp claws to help
them climb trees.

Giant pandas have five fingers
and a thumb on each paw.

The giant panda's thumb is not
a real thumb. It is a padded bone
that helps the panda
hold onto the bamboo when eating.

A baby panda is called a **cub**.

If the mother panda has two cubs, she might take care of only one.

A baby cub is born with only a thin layer of fur.

Baby pandas do not open their eyes until they are three weeks old.

When a cub is about 18 months old, it will go and live on its own.

GLOSSARY

bamboo: a species of woody, tropical grass

cub: the young of certain animals, such as the bear, wolf, or lion

endangered species: threatened with extinction

mammal: warm-blooded animals characterized by hair covering the skin and the nursing of young

wild: a place left unchanged by humans

INDEX